Stone & Thorn of Tomorrow

Stone & Thorn of Tomorrow

Today's Face of Mismanaged Democratic System

Saji Thomas

Stone & Thorn of Tomorrow

Today's Face of Mismanaged
Democratic System

Saji Thomas

Copyright © 2011 by Saji Thomas.

ISBN: Softcover   978-1-4653-7710-4
             E-book   978-1-4653-7695-4

This book was printed in the United States of America.

To order additional copies of this book, contact:
Xlibris Corporation
1-888-795-4274
www.Xlibris.com
Orders@Xlibris.com

PREFACE

I like to tell you about democracy and its importance in public management. I have given some suggestions to overcome the weakness of the democratic management. World is going behind for democracy peoples are interested to contribute their part for the development of the nation. It is important that democracy and its right effectiveness have to reach all people. But we are seeing many instance that effectiveness is not reaching to the people instead peoples are getting boring because of wrong interpretation or application of democracy.

In order to build people's confident in democracy and their active role to build our nation through democracy I am suggesting a word 'change' it may be, of our thinking, view, style of work, to adopt the new mode'. Recent days, behind of democratic administration what all are coming out, everywhere corruptions ordinary peoples are not getting justice. Let me take you some of its causes and solution.

Thank you
Saji Thomas

CONTENTS

INTRODUCTION

Democracy is a system of public management to elect his / her representative to manage and control public. The latest time democracy faces lot of challenges. Electing one representative from a group does not mean the elected one is the selection of the whole; there are other selections his / her vote may be less than 100 or 10. Election is important, to appoint one to execute the democratic management system for the public. But after we appointed one whether he / she is carrying out his duties and responsibilities in right mode of democracy? The recent corruptions, exploitations are the examples showing that there is a weakness the implementation of democratic management system.

So I am suggesting some tool to get the right effectiveness of democracy for the public, in this modern time to keep democracy in high value is very important. Failure of democracy is a major threat not only internal but it is also external. It will affect the entire growth of the country, everywhere corruptions, injustice will take place. This time every citizen of India has to re-think to initiative to build, a management tool to execute democracy without any weakness.

POLITICS

Politics is like a science for democracy to make idea. It helps the society to have democratic management and welcoming new ideas from the open group. Politics intends to bring new idea for the development of the society, nation, to protect the right of the people. It should not intend for the malpractices /exploitation / violence.

India is one of the most respected democratic countries in the world, sometimes we are thinking our democracy may be crossing the limit it is giving too much exceptions by some leaders and making a feel that leading over freedom. We are very sad to see poor moral values of our leaders especially in politics, everywhere corruptions. Why it is happening? What direction it is moving? Are we destroying the development and future of our nation? If this type of corruptions moves this way what is condition for coming generation?

Look at your window either you can see green trees / birds flying / water / you can see natural sky, just imagine if the above situation continues what you can see from your window? You will see either smoke / shutting sound / peoples running around for the help if the above situation continues. Do we need to destroy the basic concept of democracy?

Our political workers, social workers, public servants, medical person, teachers, religious people, law makers, police man, army, judge everywhere now corruption stepped-in, we these positions are holding by us, me, our father, mother, brother, sister, relatives, neighbors, uncle, aunty, our dearest friend, corruption is influenced in different form. Remember corruption is a cancer or it is serious virus of the society it will slowly destroy the entire parts of the society, e.g. it destroy human relationship, it will create violence, it will forced to give you poison, your food will be poisoned, your drinking water will poisoned, your oxygen will be poisoned etc... are the consequences of this virus.

CORRUPTION WILL DESTROY THE VALUE OF HUMAN RELATIONSHIP

What is exactly corruption? It is a type of a special interest forming a person or group of person's mind or his / her situation forced him to do a certain task. Corruption leads to kill his society or his country. Corruption could not control with a law or policy of any system or rule. It is the responsibility of the citizen to eradicate corruption from his society. If we all really interest to have a peace, healthy, safe & freedom environment, a healthy culture is an important thing.

The first step to prevent corruption a healthy culture should bring in to our country. Even though we have good back ground of culture but its molding or coating factors are getting weak because of that our cultures are getting rusty. Bharat have a very good culture, we respect our culture & believes. Then where we lose? How this virus came? If you look into our history a most common mode of living style was joint family mode if we look into the current mode there is change from joint family to nuclear family system. This change we lost the value of human relationship. A new gust came in to the picture called competition here the competition is not from a company to company, it is his brother to brother or sister to sister. What happened here? A selfish thinking or a type special interest forming to his / her head and it leads finding the ways to achieve his / her object.

The value of the human relationship is the back born to build a healthy culture. Today how to measure the value of the human relationship it is either by muscle power, money or high influence. If an elder brother is weak in financial his own younger brother may not give respect may be he will not visit his house. Personal relationship start from mother, father, children the existence of the relationship is software called love. If this love or the affection is sincere and pure, relationship will be strong and healthy this results to have trust each other. If there is trust between the people definitely will value the relationship. What is the current life style? Value of the human relationship is building by muscle power & money. Human life is highly valuable it is the gift of the God to take care his assigned task.

BIRTH GIVING SOURCE FOR INFLUENCE

We know that to get a job how much influence required? To get a school or college admission how much influence required? Not only that just live in your society you should be a member of an association / social / political organization otherwise you won't be counted. Really where we are? Where is the system? Why our citizen is not counting equal? Every day we are seeing how many associations or parties are forming with different object. Kindly review generating these association or party helping your society or you, I strongly believe it is not helping the society, it is just for the special interest of a person to achieve his own task or his group object. Nothing else, it is damaging the human relationship and trust. It may not control by law a certain extend, people has to understand and decide. People has to realize and act, again the whole power is vest with the people our administration is democratic. It is the time we should act to prevent the generation of association or political party. The more number of association or political party it is too difficult to get your justice, it lead to birth crime and corruption.

Achieving of influence in between the people most common technique is promise or offering something to a group or a society. This is the technique most commonly implementing to achieve the support of the people for an association or the political organization. I am sincerely telling you all I am not against for any particular association or a political organization, I am writing this because of sorrowing people and sad of continuous cheating mode of technique adopting to obtain the administration and control. This way peoples are cheating, developments are going away, like look at your surrounding suicide case of farmers, poor infrastructure like road, water, electricity, medical, safety of you and your family, education etc... are the example. People should realize we should not be a slave of any association or organization, when someone or association offer you any promise who is giving it? Must know he/she is the right leader can able to make it happen. Some of promises are very dangers and it is stopping your bright career or development, a type of virus injecting in to the society to bring idolism, like continuous giving of free food, selling of things below than the cost price. Its consequence or its impact is very high in the society. Just imagine if I am getting continuous free food for a long period what may happen, people may quiet his job and sit in his house why we need to work? Suppose our government is giving free food, this is seeing it by coming generation they may be not interested to do the work. Any social or government can't give free food or things less than the cost price for life long, their treasury will get empty one day and will stop all the free issues. So people has to know such promises are unhealthy it is destroying our growing future. What most commonly required a peaceful society or environment, real freedom that means without fear to travel or sleep alone anytime, anywhere? If we have such world or country really people may not use cell phone. Promise or offering should not receive from any association or organization.

Anything which is good for the society, people of that society should work together as one team regardless of any believes or different association or the member of different political idea, work to achieve the common object of the society, this is exact real brothers & sisters term of Indian culture.

INSTABILITY OF THE SYSTEM

Instability of the system, instability is a serious weakness of an individual because of it he is worrying about his and his dependent of tomorrow. This worries making him pressure, stress, temptation etc.. here he / she is forced to fail or ignore the values or believes. Many examples we can see, in day to today life monthly salary of an ordinary employee may not satisfy the requirement like his children education, sister marriage, house construction, medical treatment, take care the family etc… so what will happen he is getting pressure and bearing lot of stress that leads to lose his value. This is system failure, we must find solution. To remove the worries of an individual a strong management is to be implemented from family, village, districts to country.

Our people should always feel he have security in his ruling administration taking care of him and his / her dependent. These all could not possible to bring within a day by an individual. It is possible to bring with the hard work of every citizen. We all know that we are living in an advanced world and the distance of the world becomes very small.

We need a change to come out the from the old mode of personalized thinking, external part we have changed become more advanced now in terms of our standard of living, fashion, dress, car, house, TV, internet, cell phone, medical treatment, education, food etc.. these changes mainly where it occurred? Is it just bring only a colorful environment? Because of these changes his/her income is not sufficient, if anything running advanced means scientifically will help the human, whereas really is it helping or destroying? No doubt it is helping but we have a serious challenge because our foundation didn't rebuild to carry for the new load.

We need a change in foundation or basement, then only human will feel he will be free from worries and he will feel secure and freedom. To do a foundation change means it may be a change of approach, change of view, change of idea. Do you need safety, Security, Real freedom? If you say yes we have to accept to do a reconstruction of our foundation. We all know that more money is spending for safety and security. Look at the ruling government, are they can do something? People don't know whom to believe one side government justification, other side opposite organization's justification, what is correct? What is wrong? here people is the middle, end of the day people not getting any benefit of that promise of the plan or the project, after few days could be hearing billions or millions went to ministers or officers or agent pocket, its impact is strike, violence and destroying peoples peace and safety. In other way the one who is calling for strike and violence basically they're enjoying & sharing their happiness. This is a system failure, it is happening because of the foundation not changed according to the present living style of the world.

MANAGEMENT FOR FOUNDATION CHANGE

Foundation change can bring in to each individual but it can implement through your approach and view. Change has to take place in each individual's in his own thinking, his own approach, his own view. It has to develop with the help of some tool which can be introduced to the public from individual to his/her village, district, state and country. This type of management has to introduce by public organization which is sincerely objecting for the development of the individual and nation. If the public organization who is having right management from the top to bottom can ensure their service is reaching to the right person. What is the current system of public serving it is a fashion to make his/her name to get the influence either elected as a member of any body or local municipal, MLA, MP etc... this way going. Ordinary people always getting ignored, because of it he could not come up, his village not developing, the reason is democracy now bargaining to exist for the power to complete the term. Who is bargaining? May be your association or organization to achieve their object, here ordinary people may be will ignored or development will get ignored.

The advantage of having management tool in public organization if there is right introduction, corruption can be minimized. Easily each village level public servicing of their members can be monitored. Such organization can assure his service and presence are maintaining well. Their elective body will work effectively, if the elective administration working in right route people will get confident on their public serving organization. Issues or problems should be resolved through legally not by throwing of words or calling of strike or destroying of public propriety, this is a type of terrorism. Modern world should not support for it. This type of terrorism can be avoid or stopped only if the public system works properly.

It is the time to think every public organization / political or social workers whether you need to serve citizen or just win by promise and achieve your target. Daily victim clearly indicating that people loves right person, the one who serve for the development of the people and nation. It is the desires & dream of every citizen he/she need freedom, safety and security. To have continuous development, progress of the nation we must have a healthy environment.

Every individual is getting tired of the current mode of ruling or opposition, playing with words. People they're thinking when our organization will have time to work for our problem e.g. my village is suffering for drinking water or my village is suffering of epidemic fever or my village is facing problem of electricity whom will address this issue? Who is there to take care? Promises receiving every election but not happening, I know I am not the first person writing it but even if I am away from my nation or state or village, we 1000's of like me getting upset and sad of the things which is really going-on in our nation.

A TOOL TO MAINTAIN DEMOCRATIC MANAGEMENT

Wherever more than one person involvement or group of persons involving point there is different opinion will exist. In whatever guide line or control to bring a group to work for the common object a certain extent may succeed but it will not work long time. In front of us leaders of the political organization we are seeing throwing blames, abusing colleague of the same organization. Democratically elected leader's of public administration now blaming or putting trouble his own public servants like government employees are afraid to do his duties and responsibilities because he is not feeling security. Just imagine if the public servant not able to execute his responsibility what will be the situation of our citizen? It is the clear the indication or warning our system is reaching to that point. If it reached in a situation that public servant could not do justice, service, protection and care of the citizen, that day administration will fail.

To maintain democracy of administration a clear cut working management tool must be required. Leaders everywhere talking one subject called development of people and their city and their nation. Why the development not reaching to people? Why their cities are not developing? That means the word democracy sitting on the top of any organization but still its place is under the table of the drawer of leaders. Just making a system to vote and elect one representative from one place does not mean there is democracy or whatever opinion speaking at public or could call one day strike or making one trade union is not called for democracy.

The term democracy objects to participate or contribute or distribute idea, wealth equally to the citizen and to have a system for the public or people to listen his / her request to find a solution. He / she have freedom to express his view or opinion, his / her right to select his representative. He / she should feel confident in that system. It must ensure his / her safety & security. Democracy should have a disciplined management system to ensure the functions of democracy to carry out it in right mode. But this existing management is getting weakness, because of the corruption or mismanagement entering in democracy. It is the duty of the citizen to do strengthening our democracy. The word 'discipline' has high value in democracy, whenever the discipline violates means there is weakness in democracy.

Let me tell you in this modern world to carry out democracy its right meaning is a difficult task. If everyone who desires the right meaning of democracy, we all must change and reroute our existing basic set-up. A political theory is influenced every individual whether it right or wrong, its affection will reflect a certain extends of their working field. Every political theory have their own object it may be positive for their organizers may be will make negative impact for others. Just think about if we have 'N' number of political organization, what will be impact? This 'N' number of political organization have their own personalized object, it never made for the development of ordinary people or it never make any positive help for the ordinary political workers, it will utilize some society and will enjoy its advantage by its own organizers. The basic change is required here in people; each individual has to ask themselves do we need large number of personalized or specified object oriented organization? I like to suggest every individual should discourage forming or support to give birth for the new organization. It will be major challenges of our nation's democracy and will destroy our public administration, will destroy people development, will make unbalanced society, will rob ordinary people, will destroy your safety & security.

If our political organizations give high value and object for the people's development, people's welfare, village, Panchayat, district, state & nation, definitely corruption or other illegal things won't occur in any of the sector. Some politician is speaking party is important? What does it mean? It has to change and should say people and nation is important. Without people what is party? Organization should give high value to Protect each human life, should not justify criminal activities of political violence its impact lose of human life, it need an end.

High focus should be people and their development, organization's promise or declaration of plan is not important, its materialization or implementation is important. And people should realize it, accordingly social organizers has to work. Throwing of Personal revenge, personal blames, claims or allegation or challenge, it is not healthy for the development of nation & people. Different idea or opinion is a part of human character wherever more than one person, social workers or public servant has to work as brothers or sisters.

If we all believe the right meaning of democracy, why still we need strike? Why we need benth or harthal? If we think and ask ourselves if there is right meaning of democratic management existing with us we should not required strike or benth. Right democratic administration the most respectful position is judiciary, in case if any organization or if any government policy is against to the public interest it has to take in to judiciary in the last stage when the internal discussion fails. Properly organized democratic management should not call for strike or benth or harthal. The impact of harthal or strike or benth damaging the safety, security, freedom of the people and end fails democracy. Disagreement or disadvantage of any policy or system should express the assembly by pointing its impact or lose of the public. Any policy or system which should bring for the public must be published its all advantage and disadvantages to the public, in a democratic management people should decide accordingly system should implement. Not just only the ruling administration bringing something and fighting the oppositions putting people in confusion, this practice has to stop. Elected authority has to realize that spending capital is belongs to the people, so whatever policy or project bringing must be beneficial for the public. Development program priority should for people not the political / social organization. People is creating and strengthening the organization so people should be on the top. Political organization has to change the mode of calling strike or benth or harthal and also remember it is not a social work. Democracy is not made by threat, strike or benth or harthal, it is a threat for the public. The organization who is doing any activity against the public people should consider they do not love you. To protect the right of the citizen have high value than anything. Instead of making public facility interruption why can't approach and route issues through judiciary, which is more legal and resolve issues without interrupting public system of management.

The word of its right meaning democracy and its management will not invite any corruption and will ensure safety, security & freedom of the people. Its management tool introduction in the organization playing major role to strength democracy. It is each individual's dream to implement right democracy and it is responsibility of each citizen to make right road for the coming generation. For the right existence, healthy growth of the nation we should have healthy generation, to build it, we should prevent exploitation, selfishness & corruption, it may not resolve everything by law or any force system of control.

A transparent system of management for the public administration is important. Each citizen has to participate for the development and establishment for the best way to run democratic management. In public administration should have a common management system and continuous running of planning management without looking the color or any other means of influence. A disciplined mode of management should introduce in all the public organization. Old mode of strike, benth or harthal should avoid maximum extend, it have its own respect now it become common or personalize it is affecting citizens freedom, safety and security.

I am submitting my feelings and concerns of today and tomorrow to you. Let us hope a good tomorrow. My sincere thanks to you.

NOTES

NOTES

NOTES

NOTES

NOTES

NOTES

NOTES

NOTES

NOTES

NOTES

NOTES

NOTES